CLAY H

For Alison

CLAY HILL

TIM LIARDET

Poetry Wales Poets: 12

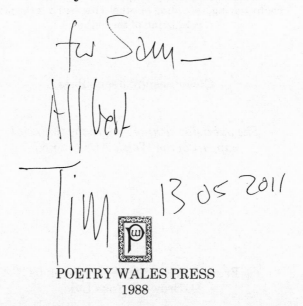

for Sam —

All best

Tim 13 05 2011

POETRY WALES PRESS
1988

POETRY WALES PRESS LTD
GREEN HOLLOWS COTTAGE, CRAIG-YR-EOS ROAD,
OGMORE-BY-SEA, MID GLAMORGAN

British Library Cataloguing in Publication Data

Liardet, Tim, *1949–*
    Clay Hill.—(Poetry Wales poets; 12).
    I. Title
    821'.914

ISBN 0-907476-88-0

Cover design: Jeane Rees

*The publisher acknowledges the financial
support of the Welsh Arts Council*

Printed in Century Schoolbook by
D. Brown & Sons Ltd.

CONTENTS

Acknowledgements

Acknowledgements are due to *Poetry Wales* and the *Anglo-Welsh Review* in which some of these poems have appeared.

I

Ashley Priory

Oppressive cloud. The municipal grass soaked
And uncut all summer. The bicyclist leans
But doesn't dismount. A few figures cross
The grass during lunchtime with wet shoes
To watch remote girls and a ball flicker
Through links of rusty wire, between the nets:
Whistling bobbling up, pumps a skittering white,
The tracksuited games-mistress shoos them off.
(The cyclist drags one boot along the wire.)

On either side, gutted houses — lifeless —
Absorb piano-scales from one classroom.
Round through its cicatrix of survival goes
The vandalised park. The light solidifies.
The suburbs of shouts and of leather taps.
The flap of heavy hair, unloading from pins.
The pea's hysteria encased in metal.

Sunnyside

(Princes Park, 1978)

The place is renowned. Detectives in the hall
Dust the latest lock.The caretaker's dreamt again
Of sandbags, smashed pianos. The drenched wall
Is caught in the pulsing of uncertain light:
The tops of the park's trees comprise her view
(The fountains beneath mossed, broken) and through
Ceilings her set elicits too much depth of bass
To decipher though it frightens the slightest fright.

The border's below. It drips. The deep South
Opens in darkness, where the exposed ground floor's
Too far from streetlamps, and mouth after mouth
Steams in the cold of a house sunk beyond its wealth.
Obstacled in deep potholes, an unlit track
Spreads into its yard, a puddled cul-de-sac
Absorbing petitions and such houses as survived
The Luftwaffe to suffer attritions of stealth.

Where it leads Law can't follow: over the glass
Of garden walls, into the park's cover, from which
Window-light retracts across the saturated grass.
Inside, a tap gasps off. Fulfilment upstairs
Disappoints an assumption of hands below.
A complaint mumbles out, while whatever can blow
With the yard's leaves down cellar steps mulches into
The one subliminal odour the whole house shares.

Dripping on faded mats — its tank's chromium
Clouding in the damp — the motorbike leant across
The hall doorway all night either keeps some-
Thing in, or out. It twists back, objectifies fear.
The place is nervous. The new tenant's antique jugs
Have been rolled up, with everything else, in the rugs.
The caretaker felt the coarse scoring diamond on
Her black glass, ploughing fibres, cutting too near:

10

She will count the darkened bulbs which ping out.
Their dim replacements light her inventory
Of angst. Mice nest in the wires. Bodies moving about
Beneath her, in whatever postures they dwell,
Match the scratching above; selfish beyond her.
She'll wake early, listening for the float's whirr
Over the potholes, jostling all that cream:
If the tits don't get it her tormentors will.

Beneath her, five dark, on four screens, grey with
     excess,
The same picture flutters exhaustedly over
And sends the same voice through the echoing house.
The pipes' soft orchestration rumbles round.
Out in the darkness, another silent car slips
Into the boating pond's slime. A long beam dips.
Crouched in a corner the latest shivering boy
Sobs in a coarse blanket. Dogs track scentless ground.

Vandries Street to Chepstow

Upstaged internal light, between caged shops,
Gathers smoke and speculation. Both grow thick.
Weightless, they rise until stopped. The stray's
Obliged by the window; it gnaws its own neck.
Shoes spread wide and shining on the steps
The grouped Jamaicans sit out the afternoon.
It is three o'clock. Leggy geldings kick
Silently at gates two hundred miles away.

One of the men gently dents his hat. The air
Of the workless siding hangs in the heat
Between meetings, and the races leave like trains,
Like mainline trains. From the run-down street
Of basements each a green avenue opening:
Long legs in mirage, ghosts against stillness,
As silent as the clatter of remote wheat.
Bright racing silks fade through heated panes.

Wedding Morning

Spenser is out but his hall clock chimes.
It grinds against distance in its hollow case.
He's far from where — the churchyard all umbrellas —
His monumental dressers endure their place.
The passage is empty that had heard him say
This was no morning to give a daughter away.

The butts pour. The lake is dark. The curtains
Are open on the rooms, gloomy beyond rain —
The family photographs, passive under glass,
Absorb the spreading moisture of the stain
Which isolates the old groups staring through
Storms that cross the farm and will continue to.

Squalls shadow his face, forty years away,
But only for an hour he has had to endure
The steamy car, and to weigh the certainty
(Through sluggish wipers that clear and blur)
His obdurate weight of body will not do
On this wedding morning what he tells it to.

The stroke surprised him, halving his strength,
The dry relatives and the floral eiderdown
Oppressed — a sourness, an incestuous sourness.
And soon he must climb steps in a rainy town
Having to watch for the splashed caps of his shoes
Strange at a distance, and to effusion effuse.

Today the lake shifts nearer to the house:
She'll speak aloud, uncertain in the airy church . . .
The cars turn in, flash back metallic light,
The umbrellas advance. And over the dirt
They swing her, and lift her train, and make
Fuss beneath which lies the level of the lake.

Ducks strain across. His drenched dogs cower
In the yard's riddled mud above which she came
To the narrow glass, a visual paleness, and left.
A lifetime drums to the sound of Summer rain
And the shell of his order waits to resume.
Confetti's a ghost fall in the silent room.

A Quiet Estate

Sir William does not like visitors.
Warnings born in his private rooms
Carry the heart's obsession out
Into depths of country quagmire,
Barb and nightshade, on a peeling board.
His dogs, his mindless dogs, are legendary.
Only the trout travel through freely.
His torch-beam scans the cellars
For the water's mark, for the danger
Of the river underneath the mill
That works upon him as it eats
At the timbers. He hates this ground,
This stony apology for ground,
Too much flint and faeces for
The bloom of his inheritance,
The vulgar weasel in under the wire.
Around him's his rearguard of staff:
Old men, in the old designations,
Securing his mind's circuitous barbs
While, far below, the water rises
Another inch and this crumbling domain
Becomes in its solitude too infested
A legacy for one gun, for a keeper
Weakening with the mortar of the hall.
Champions haunt the grassy stables
Into which the sunlight flares
Wan and emptily. The water is cold,
It swirls noisily under boards.
The old solipsist is losing his nerve.
Briars wag where ladies danced.
Ivy works its strange redress.

Rural Trilogy

Wedgwood and Saliva

Skidding on rugs, dragging the line in with them
The hunt's hounds suddenly found themselves
Into the house — fox slipping into bracken —
And snuffled round the claw-feet and antimacassars,
Duped, perplexed. Around them an amblyopia
Of dark hangings and fisheyed Victoriana.
They panted round, gonged the pendulum, tipped up,

Until they levelled out like escaping water
And exited in a gormless beating of tails.
Then Grandma jerked awake in the bathchair,
Leaning to one side, eyes suddenly bolted open,
Jaw dredging space, as the last bodeful china
Wobbled and dropped and smashed. *If it's the Skimptons,
Edie, you can wheel me into the Conservatory.*

What the Ferryman Saw

Where he rowed the ghost of a bridge was forming.
What did he see, or fancy he saw? Or didn't?
White buttocks bobbing on the other bank,
And her body all ambition, rhythmical response,
And a sloughing of clothes and a bicycle bell
Glimmering with the wide silver mirage
Of the river that noisily ran between.

And after rearrangement in silence was it
The argument, the mouths too distant for words
To be legible, the gestures clearer for that?
He slept; the ferry-bell woke him and he set out
With droplets of water dribbling from both oars.
A bonnet bobbed at the bows; the woman beneath
Rocked gently in the wake still wearing it.

Hitting Straight

Doctor Jack could hit. (A clean elation
Somewhere outlasts the ease of the springs.)
Bank Holiday, 1909, he lofted the Castle's spinner
Over the Parish Hall, a hit never equalled.
Up it went, threatening Pritchard's greenhouses.
Three hundred panes, and not one chosen!
No yell! No crash! The players thrashed about

In the long grass, by which time the ball
Had probably plopped into the shady Ceiriog
And crossed the border into England, either
Startled timid Friesians with reverberant thud
Or someone sleeping open-mouthed beneath
A handkerchief, cup a-tilt. *Only God and It
Knew where it landed. Well, they kept the secret.*

Notes for Emmeline Worthy

Squat humourless woman with the weak eyesight,
(Her leitmotif a skidding anthem of chairs)
Tight armpits damp, speaker without largesse,
When she clapped chalk and sat her voice resumed
The old recycle of words her spectacles
Adjusted to page and sense, linking up cadences
Through the slow pollination of the afternoon.
Radiators cold in Summer. The skinned torso
Shamelessly displayed on the board above her,
Rabbit or human, dust in its squashed roll.

Blood distends the pinis. Response pressure-cooked
In a prospect of blouses secreting their changes,
The growing pressure beneath them altering
The shape of mouths, amongst voices cracking open
In mulish ululations, Harvey with brightened acne
Squeezing in his pocket. Mouth yoked to something
Years old she chewed two stringy syllables,
Or held the word away perhaps like a dead mouse
To make it less flavoursome, less mouse, less what
Father Worthy might attempt to do with his.

All gleams and flitting bits without those spectacles.
. . . *Millions of spermatozoa swim up the pinis.*
Annelids squelched against glass, stick-insects
Reverted, amongst bunsens, the faint smell of gas,
As the next drip unclung and splashed in the depths.
Blank cartridge received our limp replicas
Of Leonardo. Out beneath the low ceiling
In the heat of the field the mild donkey
Withdrawing from flies at the chain's limit throughout
The lesson extruded its cooling member.

Henry George Lumm's Kinetoscope

(Four sorts of removal from grief)

1

The aged Himalayan monkey unwound its tail.
The regiment team grossed the long afternoon.
You bequeathed it me; the frayed, misshapen ball,
Grandfather, only your fingers could spin.

2

Death's bodyweight, men becoming pistons, thrown
Against the caked gun, against mud that bears
Iron and equine strength and drenched khaki down.
(And all the bruised hands identical to yours.)

Shoulders on the felloes; neither east nor west
Ahead or behind, the sky's billowing borne
Closely over backs and the Ancre's crawled waste.
(All the cracked nails, as yours, rivelled as horn.)

3

You got out alive; gassed, sent south. A chain
Of blind hands grasped shoulders, seams of braille,
And somewhere in the layers of every man
Who hunched round a mug in a waterlogged hole

Darkness drenched to greater weight blent your own,
The windy pier, etcetera. The muck each trod
Assailed you. (Your whiteness exposed the line
Exposed by each throat and unhelmeted head.)

And Rheims' sandbags, piled up, hardened to stone,
Against the great cathedral door were anchorage:
Smothered by leaf-gas the barges drifted down
Thudding against the wall's moss, your old age.

4

The buds erected, sticky with afterbirth.
The polish bubbled up where the heat sealed in;
In hissing soft explosions the knots broke forth;
(Your holocaust was your reunion.)

Clay Hill

(1867-1971)

1

The sorrel reseeded, the scorched,
Dilapidated holly dropped down
Underneath its own weight into
Clattery heaps, metallic sheen dulled
By Summer dust, such exequies.
You gone grandfather, the order
Bulged over its paths, the lilac's
Oppressive shade slowly deepening
Its acoustics for the wren's pipes
Absorbed the pursuit of an impulse
From lilac to shed, shed to lilac,
The frail collapsible furrows
Of discarded tin, frilled with rust,
To asphalt's boiling interior.
When the ancient lease was unearthed
In its murk of text, withholding
A catchment of mouse-dirt and clung to
By the glue spoon, in a damp drawer,
The contractors could alter all
The angles of the shadows at last:
And it was left to scratched chasses
To drag balled wire and clear new lines
Of vision, breaking the dark meshes
That locked for a moment and softly
Crackled apart, releasing the sweet
And the mulled and secreted odours
Of ripped shrub-bark, the gnostic saps,
The stored faith which released at last
The family hold in clouds of seed.

2

Steeped in your father's example,
A hundred years of clutter was
Stuck there, subtly balanced, amongst
Old shrubbery, warming pebbledash,
Suspended like the decision
To stay or to leave, never made.
The last, the very last, of Flanders'
Stones were finally flushed out with
The mud clinging to your hobnails:
You gone, your Emily following,
The whole place relapsed by degrees
To a childhood restorative,
To a toddling forth, amid clearings,
Restrained by Victorian reins.
A soft alacrity dithered there.
Blowing diesel and phlox about
Itself, and settling, at length,
To a puttering on, or to the scratch
Of hurled round gravel the future
Burst through the back of the shed.

Warringer and Aggy

(Erbistock, 1937)

The vision returned. The respectful ostlers
With hands held folded. The Slaughterhouse cart
And the squealing of the winch as the mare
Was lifted, her lids sliding off her eyeballs.
When the head bouldered back the great molars
Dropped open and shut, producing the noise
Which unnerved all the uncapped stable-boys.

Was it death's own hollow rumination,
The beyond of the peristalsis? A rumour
Of calcium moved through the hierarchy
Of grinning greyhound skulls into which orchard
She would not be lowered, passive as she was
To the abattoir's chains, beneficent to
The covert backroom formulas of glue.

He kept the stud-book, the groom, sealing her line
Of temperamental ghosts and thoroughbreds.
Those cocksure and those violent suitors
Sparked on the cobbles. Their eccentric names
Sired the greedy mouths of stumbling champions
To exhaust the ancient gateway of her blood.
His heart's lawns trundled to each dull stamping thud.

The pump gave out; hounds sent up steam and whine.
For years he would attempt to carve the shape
Of her shapeless turmoil in the barn's lamps.
The crystals of her sweating death clung to his hands
As her afterbirth had, confusing as they did
The mysteries of church-Latin with the heads
Of beasts carved in wood or the splashes on the leads.

In the swilled gullies, her viscera unravelled
Like giant sardines, packed for function, muscles and
        joints
Still working but of the mare nothing at all.
The knife's deftness bore the grim tutelage
Which possessed him. Strung up in its sinews
The soul aborted. Appalled by its flayed flesh he
Tripped on the gurgling grids of old Ontology.

Stigmata

(Kinmel Park Transit Camp, March, 1919)

1

After France's mud for the dumped Canadians
The mud of Denbighshire, sucking at their puttees
And boots; just extricated, bulled for return.
Dock and home receded, flags and laden trams,
Such seedburst. While other trains got home
They were shunted out towards the dead-end
Of Ypres' depressing siding, the camp's half-world
Of the repetitious shedding of the moody rain
And remoteness of bleary coastal lights
To whose unheavenly promise one line led out.
After France's mud, delay, the arsehole
Of a Welsh winter and the Quartermaster's nibs,
The thought of the great rainy Atlantic dividing.

Optical light. Occlusion. The submerged duck-boards
Bringing them back only to the commonplace
Of themselves, the smell of males in huts
Oppressed by their own animal repetitions
And recycled breath and impotence to move at all,
Without heat, pay. "The situation will be . . .", etcetera.
The daily evocations of army typewriters
Clacked against them, worse trenches than the
        trenches.
This was not the hoarse voice on the field-telephone
— Tapped though utterly dead — getting no answer
And thinning itself until disembodied.
Dampness seeped deeper, their blanketed heaps
Snaffled by influenza, booking the whole churchyard.

2

Too close to France's clouds, the undrained terrain
With every cloying boot-load of it symbolised
Beautiful gratitude. A prurient local culture
Compounded the wire, the limits contracting.
When the riot broke — flames seen from as far as Rhyl,
The shopkeepers of Abergele boarding up —
The British regiment was instructed, and sent in.
Five Canadians dead by cold light. Laid out
In the rain the human bodies seemed too slight
For such catharsis, punched through like buckets, as if
The bayonets had opened up more than flesh.
Stretcher-bearers resoiled their boots. The spokes
Of the field-ambulance picked up mud and slapped it
      back.

I'd seen wounds, but such as these — bayonet driving
The throat's muscles out through the back of the head —
Flesh burned to a charred star by close aiming —
Argued deeper resentment, something half understood,
As if to say these foreigners, being confined,
Had brought too near a fancy for white breasts
Under buttons only we might undo, or failed
To scrape boots and begrimed an affected threshold
With too much unaffected ease, as if at home.
The British tried to trap the outcome in between
The trained sidling horse-flanks of official displacement,
Clopping up lanes, unspooling from their spurs
The godawful winter of the playful summer.

The constables pulled on their caps. After four years
Of foreign mud that never was quite brought in,
Of poachers in bicycle lamps, the comfort of dry socks,
The Constabulary was getting cocky again,
Brushing down its uniforms, ink in its pads,
Smelling the murders like pork after rationing.
Beyond the leather creaks of any doodling Court
The ditched Canadians were shunted out quick.
At Liverpool's dockside ensued a galvanic
Dumping of grain and design. Troopships became
Troopships again. The Coroner's Inquest, well,
Postponed. The Canadians were blamed. The banshee
Of the truth fled from itself, finding protection.

Open-necked, unshaven, let no man mistake by whom
The five with mortuary-tags tied to their toes
Under the cloud cover of peacetime were used.
Pale translucence drawn to tendrils of smashed veins —
Ganglions of obscene intrusion, strained wrists —
Reproved the prophylaxis of British Lee-Enfields
Still waking the sweating minister sixty years ahead.
Rainwater, waxed youth. We must assume something
        needed
Bayonet-holes through which to bleed. The victims
Were five in twelve million, drawn down after all
With Europe's ironmongery, a fivefold baring of heads
Of matted hair that could not be covered up
By five greatcoats, stained by such fresh springs of
        turmoil.

Retreat, 1982

Glimpsed at a distance, a hundred yards off,
They are the latest tenants to inherit
The place's silence, its draughts and foibles
And eroded bricks reappearing through whitewash,
The violent cracks in its outhouse walls.
Into the baked yard of that dense approach's
Tidal shifts of foliage few visitors come.
Only one granching hatchback regularly
Leaves and returns, refinding its own tracks
To the squealing of briars against dull tin.

Balking at privacy, when space had been made,
After six months all conjecture concerning
This private, unsociable couple, living with
Books and themselves across three ill-drained fields
Of dissipated streams, trickling into marsh,
Declined for want of nourishment or noise.
Around them old homes hug the dead incursion
Of the closed line, whose silence delimits
One boarded halt, a scrub of iron linking
Sociable tongues to defunct cattle trucks.

Identified in each other, and childless,
Stripped back to necessity, to rent and fuel,
They preserve seclusion, like a sort of power:
Reports of nakedness on the lighted lawn
Go with the mail. The distant road's traffic
Thickens twice a day, and sunk in dappled fathoms
The gate implies inhabited, and by whom:
Old, creepered in privacy, the monastery wall
Of the sycamores preserves what by now
Is only the silted residue of mystery.

Gas

"That was a dark night, all the women
Blown with the rain and whipped lamps
At the pit-head, tugging the cage . . . confusion.
Anyone who says he's not afraid of
Gas is a liar, but we are not
Strangers to faith."

Adjusting delicately throughout
He kept his eyes, fixed through binoculars,
On the panting ewe across the field.
                                        "She'll
Deliver in a moment, you see."
His earlobe was black with the peat
From fingering the pots in the greenhouse.
                                        "We
Gathered where space was made in the yard,
The exhausted brigade, arranged
For the press, our hair sleeked, wretched
As Scott at the Pole. The rest? Abandoned.
Lost beyond the billowing wall of
Gas which stopped us, bulging out
Of its seems and scorching our singlets
As far beneath the church-floor in yards
As the Parish spire rose above it in feet . . ."
He stared across the sunlit field.
                                        "Here
Comes the little bugger now."

Psychosis

The lamps' pouring tunnel, darkness at speed,
The white repetitious flash and the wipers
Striving mechanically, though overwhelmed.
Ivy and towering trees, too old for concern,
Flee from the beams which meet and climb past
The houses, all doors shut and all lights out,
As the wet white glare of the farm wall lunges

Down, and still further below, swollen with rain,
The Ceiriog leaps and roars on its way,
Dragging its black weeds, mad and preoccupied.
I drive into the turbulence of driven rain
As uneasy of my relation to it as
The river's black weeds are to the turbulence
Thundering through them, all that rough water

Driving the stones with which everything flies.
The frogs gleam in the lamps, along the way,
Up from river-mud to the mindless instinct
They obey as if it is something almost —
The ogling pike with its brains thrashed out —
Demanding immolation. The lane's tarmac leaps
In mesmerisms. It will lead me round its bends

To the lighted box. Back through darkness — in the
arms
Of her sister, on cushioned springs, subsumed
By all that makes her perpetually shiver —
A young woman fears that her mind will follow
Her aborted foetus. Frogs climb the wet banks
To a dangerous surface. The black foam romps.
The preoccupied valley cannot send a doctor.

The Fog Before the Frogmen

What swung through us wildly was the line
Of fear's demarcation, all safe beyond,
A centreless contour corralling danger.

Not that the helicopter's invisible blades
Came close enough to set the grass eddying,
Or that the pilot in his earphones was not

As featureless and eyeless as any
Robotic impulse when he turned away
In his own eerie wind, heading back.

Five miles upcountry a breathing line of men
Thrashed its way up the foggy incline,
Leaving the pillbox clear, the canal tunnel.

(There were reports of the maniacal staring
Of a running man the squealing car bounced round,
Hands to bonnet, chest heaving, lurching off.)

Lamps bobbed in the woods, as the line broke order
Towards the river, searching for the strap
Of a sandal, or the cuff of a windcheater,

Or the glimpse of an ankle sock or wellington
Or the billowing red of an oilskin turning to elude
Its lodging-place and drift, toward the weir.

What we saw, what in the end barely touched us,
Was the silent storm of the helicopter's
Power, equipped — sinisterly remote —

Out on the very boundary and crumbling edge
Of a mother's grief, of a mother bent
Double over the clasped void of her child.

II

Letters Home

1

Your dark pupils moving across the ceiling,
In a silence of ritual preparation
For sleep, another temporary ceiling,
Trace the shadows' vagaries, cracks: a window.
So unnecessitous your earnest strength.
Ceilings gather, veined with likelihood at length.

2

Your body's itself; expunging the last signs
Of clothing, after the warmth of the water.
Such weight of hair pinned, your arms gathering
Towel to raised foot. Where your spine moves
Sunlight balks, then flows again; it and the steam,
Which is which? Both harness every gleam

Of chromium taps and old enamelled iron.
They find you in your singleness of flesh.
When you move you induct such delicate displays
Of dust, the silent coruscating drifts
Of silver, every particle and spark,
Utterly symphonic, shoal-passive; your own work.

3

The tussocks make the mower nag and moan.
You walk your head out of view in the sun
Then show me your back until you turn at the top,
Intent, chewing your lip, hating mowing.
To see you when you think no one is watching you:
I do not call to you from here, but do.

At Nannerch

Crossing the glared white garden,
At the house's open French windows
We stop — talk suspended — hearing
A child's voice from the upper room's
Depth, half in sleep, half returned;
A resumption, a waking, of need.

Windless air, the birds — everywhere
The lineaments of drought — intervene:
We pause, father, mother, grandmother,
Under the sill's edge of that voice,
On the bleached lawn, about to enter,
Arranged a certain distance apart.
The dresser's oversized brilliance
Of mirror, reversing the lot, returns
Through the vagueness of the room
Its silent masterpiece of nuance.

Summer Storm

1

The pressure quadruples. Insects beneath it
Crawl under each leaf. The guttering's spider
Wobbles its rigging. Old and immense
The sycamores gather — all stillness and resignation —
The shallows of their gloom upon which
The Toby Jugs squander a puffed glance
Creep indoors. No lights. The dark garden's
Abandoned mowing maroons its ragged island
As the clock beats strong, against the Approach.

The fields are sensuous, rank with odours.
Out of the distance — suddenly overhead —
The firmamental boulders are being
Tipped, disgruntled, grumbling round.
One electrical suture splices down.
The first hesitant drops plip on the glass
Like the moths, their inearthly eye-lights
Blundering against a curtailed obstruction.
One ungainly duck flaps panicking up
Across the gloom caught in sudden daylight.
The trough bubbles. Each leaf begins to bounce.

My tongue found your wetness at last.
Spread wide, breasts lapsing back, eyes shut
And head to one side — hair spread on a surface
As if on water, as if perfectly weightless —
You lay above, warm feathers settling round you.
All lights gone, whatever remained of the storm
Moved around us and the open-curtained room
In which we moved together almost eerily
By its eerie light, your feet in the air
And toes straining up, to fetch our noises
From their submerged-places through our scorched
      throats.
The broken-hedged fields of flattened hay
Out under the sycamores flashed in the last
Innocuous spasms, framed by the window,
Shadowing the tensed vertebrae along my spine.
Belly to belly, moisture into moisture.

Pubescent Dream of the Baths

I'm changed, but someone else's water pools
The cubicle floor. The muffled whistle fills
The chamber that fills a larger chamber
Whose balustrades look down but is it upon
The lane-lines wobbling gently underwater,
Waiting to be shattered? The echo dies, then peeps
      again.

I smell the chlorine, but see nothing, straining up
At the air-vent as the girls begin to slip
Into their costumes, and though I sense bare heels
Thudding dully and know they're on their way
(Pulling down caps, carrying bright towels
Or adjusting elastic, heads up and orderly

With unbroken stride, cross-swinging arms . . .)
From the vent I glimpse nothing. Only the forms
And a clean elongated perspective of tiles
And glossed water pipes holding pressure inside
Suggestions of sweat, the parallel rails
Growing labyrinthine, wherever they lead.

I strain at the air-vent for more height. The noise
And spaciousness of the pool (not for boys)
— Where perhaps the bobbing floats' flotilla
Directs a white refractive foam of feet
And g-forcing thighs — grows gradually smaller
And more distant, audible, but out of sight.

Under Upper Tier

To avoid the glazed queues at Tea
I trouble the row between Overs,
To assuage fermenting discomfort,
The gaseous contents of the can . . .
Cracked tiles, shall we say, map relief.

A gloom behind the sunlit field.
As sudden as the jets that flush
Away, in the stand above, the roar
Of ruptured concentration, a span
Underneath clattering with fresh claps.

And I know that someone (walking back
Feeling perhaps the ghost of the ghost
Of the dead thud on the pad) is out.
His mood, checked for cameras, matches
My single overwhelmed expletive.

He walks from sunlight to the gloom.
I walk from the gloom to sunlight.
A ball blurred. Above me consensus
Gathers like the amplified sound
Of rainfall. Grass warms. Cisterns hiss.

Extension 101

You hear my unsolicitous voice on the line
Through interference, mid-morning static.
The switchboard bobs in. With renewed taste
Of insipid dislike you recall my name.
Voices wimple, distant. A tap squeals
Through its worn washer. A word stifles.
You hear my voice, but do not hear it —
The noise, say, of someone else's radio
Or of energetic plumbers ustairs,
Both reduced by walls but irritating
When you want to concentrate exclusively
On your own noise, or perhaps to water
That old and dessicated resting-place
Of parched errata, or to watch in between
That loose falling away of blouse reveal
Even more than yesterday's, or to see if
The pensioner snipping unhurriedly at
His topiary, three floors down in the sun,
Has turned the corner of his prim hedge;
So that you can see the flash of shears
Still clipping upside down along the top
But no cap, no pensioner, his progress
Measuring the warmed yards and passing of
A morning stunted by its caffeic want,
And bringing ever nearer the Trolley's
Squeaky salvation. Am I misinformed?
I had asked for the Section Manager
And they plugged me to you or rather
Plugged me about then plugged me to you.
The vents judder on. But it is too hot
To barter for adjectives down this line.
The temperature rises. Your jacket is off
Above a country town jammed with traffic.
You are in error. Your latest figures are
A sardonic nonsense, wonky in a heatwave,

Like the heat below off crammed bonnets,
The fumy will-o'-the-wisp of gasoline,
Or a mirage of tourists. By the time you
Have begun to commit to paper what I say
Through the hollow miniature conduit
Of your chewed biro's length it has become
Something only conduits can dispose of —
A mile above the town the estuary slowly
Withdraws from its gulled and trickling mud.
The pavement's all clippings. The trolley's
Stuck in the lift where silver pots stew.
A shoal-chorus of exercised fingers
Responds to the morning's invisible tide.

The Reading Room

Over the darkened town, in the boiling ward,
You hold hour old flesh to your sensitive flesh
Behind curtains, encrimsoning in the warmth
Of a strange jurisdiction, having fused the need
And the gift of water warm and paradisial.
Duly exiled to freezing streets whose shops
Test alarms and drop shutters I kill an hour
In the Reading Room, as if between trains,
Attempting to keep warm amongst others as
Temporary, in overcoats, crackling the papers.

This dingy public hall of evening draughts
And tepid heaters, ladders to creaky heaven,
Succumbs to the room more private, in which
Your long arms draw me back into the range
Of your physical stress, where I steady to hold:
I feel under my hands the length of your spine
Arch up and over, as if you were crawling
Backwards up a tunnel, half hearing voices,
Winding your body back, half brutal, half gentle,
Over his drenched hair, squeezed convolutions —

Shades cast little pools on marked surfaces.
I watch the faces, above books, some spectacled —
All the gestures. Somebody is whispering on
The landing. A request descends. The fanned pages
Flicker and the room responds to creaks if not
To your passionate nearness. Even in this locus
Of human separation, our bodily embrace holds
And refuses to break, a silence boomed against
By book-boards and by coughs takes back with them
The subversive humour of our exultation.

Joseph Climbing

The old stair-treads softly protest, as you
Start to heave yourself up towards the landing:

Encrustations of old gloss (where chipped white
Exposes the turquoise exposing the green)

Overload the mouldings, on each side, along
Which you feel a way for the place to grip,

A year old, testing each flexible taut leg
Against its own hinge, and in baggy leggings

Bend into the effort, grunting and happy,
Flatfooting dazzling plimsolls so much that

Your rear-end, packed to absorb, sways higher
Up in air than your head, following you.

Around to the door's bright thawing blebs
Of glass, in the winter gloom of the stairwell,

You turn slowly, with a wild freedom of smile,
Your face illuminated, confirming I follow.

And turn to resume, unaware that although
I crouch to catch, you make the climb alone,

And that a time will come I will not follow;
Excited by height, breathing steam, and squealing,

You approach the landing's steep emergence
Of cupboard, the surprise of echo rebounding.

And exhilarated there, you pause to scrub up
The pert flowers out of the carpet's pattern.

Joseph's Fairground

Amongst it is to be found, you teach me, the world
Beneath the counter-level of the Hamburger Van.

A noisy undertow sucks. I put you down
Onto your feet. You sway, pause. A hesitant intake.
A combined bolt towards and withdrawing away.
                     Barrur. Shnsta. Old boards
Undulate, rattling round — Black Sambo's Tigers

Carried aloft. Groga. Groga. Groga. Groga.
Greased chains and pullies, the swingeing monsters
Clash in shadows. And which particular song
To listen to, so many competing at once
For one auditorium, amongst grumbling generators?

It is the world into which the great sumps
Of fairground lorries drip their dark oil.

Where massed cables lock beneath sandals
And make you fall, stumbling forward. What is it you
      dream
And will recall? The toy you carry rolls
From your reach, and you wish to retrieve it.

Shadows revolve over you, huge and symmetrical,
Dependent on one centre. A poured blurring
Of people goes round, visible through a crack
Between two sections of awning which configure
One gigantic face, insatiable and mindless:

Ankles caught in the dead weight of the skeins
Of insulated power, you glimpse for a moment
The great axle revolving beneath, hemmed in canvas
Where it holds everything up, grinding the grist
Of its grease, and flinging screams, like sparks.

Note

Stigmata: The events of March, 1919, at Kinmel Park Camp have remained something of an enigma for sixty years, in spite of their parochial notoriety.

The historiography of the riots is weak and there seems to be a reluctance in many quarters to speak openly about them. It is widely regarded, however, that the Canadian soldiers, depressed and frustrated by incessantly postponed repatriation dates, squabbled amongst themselves, duly causing the deaths of five of their own number as a result of bullet-and bayonet-wounds. In the monologue, an anonymous observer, possibly a doctor — drawn from the researches and memories of various undisclosable sources — relates the events as he understands them.